Guided Reading Notes

White Band
Oxford Level 10

Inventors and Inventions

Contents

Introduction	2
Underwater Adventure (Fiction)	6
Cuckoo Trouble (Fiction)	13
Ant and the Break-bot (Fiction)	20
Flying Machines (Non-fiction)	27
Extreme Exploring Machines (Non-fiction)	34

Introduction

Why is guided reading important?

Guided reading plays an important role in your whole-school provision for reading, providing opportunities for children to progress and develop the key competencies they need to become confident and skilled independent readers. Working with small groups of children, with texts closely matched to the readers' needs, guided reading is the perfect vehicle for delivering focused teaching from Reception/PI right through to Year 6/P7. The teacher-pupil interaction also provides a valuable assessment opportunity, helping you identify exactly what each child can and can't do. Through guided reading children also encounter a world of exciting, whole books – building a community of readers who read for pleasure.

About *Project X Origins*

Project X Origins is a comprehensive, whole-school guided reading programme designed to help you teach the wide range of skills essential to ensure children progress as readers and to help nurture a love of reading.

Ensuring the key skills are covered

Project X Origins incorporates all of the key skills children need to develop to become successful and enthusiastic readers:

> **Word reading:** phonically regular and common exception words are introduced systematically in the early levels with phonic opportunities provided throughout the notes. As children progress, they are encouraged to use their decoding skills whenever they encounter new or unfamiliar words, and also to recognize how this impacts on different spelling rules.

> **Comprehension:** understanding what has been read is central to being an effective and engaged reader but comprehension is not something that comes automatically so specific strategies have been built into the notes to ensure children develop comprehension skills they can use over a range of texts:

- Previewing
- Predicting
- Activating and building prior knowledge
- Questioning
- Recalling
- Visualizing and other sensory responses
- Deducing, inferring and drawing conclusions
- Determining importance
- Synthesizing
- Empathizing
- Summarizing
- Personal response, including adopting a critical response

> **Reading fluency:** fluency occurs as children develop automatic word recognition, reading with pace and expression. Strategies to help achieve this, including meaningful opportunities for oral reading, re-reading and re-listening are provided throughout.

> **Vocabulary:** introducing new vocabulary within a meaningful context is an important element in extending children's vocabulary range, developing their reading fluency and comprehension. Each thematic cluster provides opportunities for revisiting and reinforcing vocabulary over a range of books and contexts.

> **Grammar, punctuation and spelling:** learning about language in the context of a text, rather than through a series of discrete exercises, can help make grammar, punctuation and spelling relevant and helps children make the link between grammar, punctuation and clarity of meaning, thus supporting their development as writers. Opportunities to support an in-depth look at language are provided for every book from Year 1/P2 to Year 6/P7.

> **Spoken language:** talk is crucial to learning and developing their comprehension so children are given plenty of opportunities to: discuss and debate their ideas with others; justify their opinions; ask and answer questions; explore and hypothesise; summarise, describe and explain; and listen and respond to the ideas of others.

Assessment and progression in reading

Project X Origins includes a rigorous assessment spine drawn from the *Oxford Reading Criterion Scale* to ensure that you know exactly what each child can do and what they need to focus on next in order to make progress. This assessment framework, combined with the careful levelling of the Oxford Levels, will help you select the right book with the right level of challenge for each of your guided reading groups and to assess, track and monitor each child's progress.

Step 1

On a termly basis, use the *Oxford Reading Criterion Scale* (which can be found in the relevant *Project X Origins Teaching Handbook*) to assess each child's reading. The scale will tell you the Oxford Level a child is comfortable reading at, and the areas a child needs to develop. You can also use this assessment to form your guided reading groups.

Step 2

Plan your guided reading sessions by selecting books at the appropriate Oxford Level that focus on the relevant learning needs of the group. You will find charts showing the learning objectives and assessment points for every *Project X Origins* book in the relevant *Project X Origins Teaching Handbook*. Depending on your assessment, you might choose a book at the level the children are comfortable at or one from the next level up, to offer some stretch.

Step 3

Use the assessment points within the Guided Reading Notes to support on-going assessment of children's reading progress. The Progress Tracking Charts in the relevant *Project X Origins Teaching Handbook* can be used to record this if you wish. Regularly re-assess each child's progress combining your on-going informal assessments and the termly assessment using the *Oxford Reading Criterion Scale*. Use this information to re-organize guided reading groups and teaching plans in response to children's varying degrees of progress.

Getting started: using the Guided Reading Notes

At a glance
Project X Origins Guided Reading Notes offer detailed guidance to help deliver effective and engaging guided reading sessions, and are designed to be used flexibly to ensure you get the most out of each book. For notes containing multiple sessions, you may choose to focus on each of these sessions or focus on one session and have the children read the rest of the book independently.

Curricular correlation and assessment
At the beginning of every set of notes there are correlation charts for all UK curricula, ensuring that across the clusters the main curricular objectives are covered. In addition, an overview of assessment points for each book is provided – these points are also signposted throughout the notes.

Key information
Before the first session, an overview of the book and the resources you will need (such as additional photocopy masters) is provided.

Teaching sequence
Each guided reading session follows the same teaching sequence:
- **Before reading**: children explore the context of each book to support their understanding and help them engage with the text. They are encouraged to discuss, recall, respond, predict and speculate about the book. Opportunities to focus on word reading and/or vocabulary are also introduced at this point.
- **During reading**: children are given a section of the book to read with specific questions in mind.
- **After reading**: children reflect on and discuss what they have read. They are encouraged to delve deeper, exploring their understanding of the text, developing their vocabulary, grammar, punctuation, spelling and fluency where appropriate.
- **Follow-up**: opportunities for children to extend their learning outside the session are provided, including writing and cross-curricular activities.

Throughout the sessions, the key strategies that children are developing are clearly identified.

Underwater Adventure
BY TONY BRADMAN

Curricular correlation

English National Curriculum

Spoken language	Consider and evaluate different viewpoints, attending to and building on the contributions of others
Word reading	Read accurately by blending the sounds in words that contain the graphemes taught so far, especially recognising alternative sounds for graphemes
Comprehension	Recognise simple recurring literary language in stories
	Make inferences on the basis of what has been read so far
	Predict what might happen on the basis of what has been read so far

Phonics and vocabulary

GPCs	/er/ perfect, certain, surface, urgently, clockwork, first /oo/ room, cuckoo, zoom, super, lose, through
Decodable 2 and 3 syllable words	hanging, metal, airlock, clockwork
Common exception words	going, can't, cried, because, would, we're, looking, park
Challenge and context words	submarine, periscope, water-beetle, cuckoo, murky, tangled, antique, touch, machine, break, build, larvae

Grammar, punctuation and spelling

Grammar and Punctuation	Correct choice and consistent use of present tense and past tense throughout writing	Ant carefully opened the box. He took out a small machine. "This is our latest invention," …
Spelling	The /l/ sound spelt -al at the end of words	metal, pedal, special, dial

Reading assessment points (Oxford Reading Criterion Scale: Assessment Standard 3)

1. Can the children identify when reading does not make sense and self-correct in order for the text to make sense? (READ)
7. Can the children make predictions about a text using a range of clues? (D)
20. Having read a text, can the children find the answers to questions, both written and oral? (R)
21. Can the children talk about how different words and phrases affect meaning? (E)
23. Are the children beginning to read between the lines, using clues from text and pictures, to discuss thoughts, feelings and actions? (D)

Scottish Curriculum for Excellence

Listening and talking	I can show my understanding of what I listen to or watch by responding to and asking different kinds of questions LIT 1-07a
Reading	I can use my knowledge of sight vocabulary, phonics, context clues, punctuation and grammar to read with understanding and expression ENG 1-12a
	I can share my thoughts about structure, characters and/or setting, recognise the writer's message and relate it to my own experiences, and comment on the effective choice of words and other features ENG 1-19a
	To show my understanding, I can respond to different kinds of questions and other close reading tasks and I am learning to create some questions of my own ENG 1-17a

Foundation Phase Framework in Wales

Oracy	Express opinions, giving reasons, and provide appropriate answers to questions (Speaking)
	Show understanding of what they have heard by asking relevant questions to find out specific information (Listening)
Reading	Apply the following reading strategies with increasing frequency to a range of familiar and unfamiliar texts: phonic strategies; recognition of HFW; context clues, e.g. prior knowledge; graphic and syntactic clues; self-correction, including re-reading and reading ahead (Reading strategies)
	Show understanding and express opinions about language, information and events in texts (Response and analysis)
	Express views about information and details in a text (Response and analysis)

Northern Ireland Curriculum

Talking and Listening	Devise and ask questions to find information in social situations and across the curriculum
Reading	Use a range of strategies to identify unfamiliar words
	Explore and begin to understand how texts are structured in a range of genres
	Express opinions and give reasons based on what they have read

Underwater Adventure

7

Underwater Adventure

About this book

Tiger loses his watch in the pond in the park. Luckily, Max and Ant have been working on a new invention – a Super Micro-Submarine. They dive to the bottom of the pond to rescue the watch but all does not go to plan.

You will need

- *Prediction and reflection grid* Photocopy Master, *Teaching Handbook* for Year 2/P3
- *First and third person words* Photocopy Master, *Teaching Handbook* for Year 2/P3
- *My invention* Photocopy Master, *Teaching Handbook* for Year 2/P3

▶ Before reading

- Ask the children to notice who is on the front cover. Where are Max and Ant? (underwater) **(activating prior knowledge)**
- What sort of adventures might they have underwater? **(predicting)**
- Read up to page 6 to the children. Talk to them about the story so far. Point out that it seems to have nothing to do with being underwater. **(previewing the text)**
- How do they think this section might lead into an underwater adventure? **(predicting)**
- Ask the children what to do if they encounter a difficult word, modelling with an example from the book.
- Discuss with the children what to do if they struggle to understand the meaning of a word or a sentence, e.g. rereading the word or sentence again.

Assessment point

Can the children make predictions about a text using a range of clues? (ORCS Standard 3, 7)

Assessment point

Can the children identify when reading does not make sense and self-correct in order for the text to make sense? (ORCS Standard 3, 1)

> *Phonic opportunity*

- Draw attention to words with the /**er**/ phoneme: *perfect, certain, surface, urgently, clockwork, first*. Ask the children to identify the GPC /er/ in the words. Support children to say each phoneme and then blend the phonemes to read the word.
- Now look at words with the /**oo**/ phoneme: *room, cuckoo, zoom, super, lose, through*.
- Alternatively, depending on the phonic work you have been undertaking, select one or two of the words from the book and remind the children how to say and blend phonemes.
- You may also wish to point out some of the common exception words or practise decoding some of the challenge and context words in this book.

During reading

- Ask the children to read from page 7 to the end of the book.

After reading

Returning to the text

- How did Tiger lose his watch? **(recall)**
- Why does Ant say to Tiger: *"We wouldn't want you to break anything"*? **(deducing, inferring, drawing conclusions)**
- How do they think Tiger feels when the other children say he might break things? **(empathizing)**
- Why do they think the cuckoo clock might be important to the story? **(synthesizing, deducing, inferring, drawing conclusions)**

Assessment point
Having read a text, can the children find the answers to questions, both written and oral? (ORCS Standard 3, 20)

Developing comprehension

- Ask the children, in small groups, to create a freeze frame image of the last scene in the book, where Max and Ant are trapped in the submarine whilst Cat and Tiger are at the edge of the pond. Tap the children on the shoulder and ask them to describe what they are thinking. Once they have shared their thoughts in role, let them explore the next story through role play. What do they think will happen next? How will Tiger help them out of their sticky situation? **(personal response, determining importance, predicting)**

- Ask the children to fill in the *Prediction and reflection grid* Photocopy Master to consider what might happen in the next book (*Cuckoo Trouble*). They can fill in the last section when they read *Cuckoo Trouble*. **(deducing, inferring, predicting)**

> **Assessment point**
> Are the children beginning to read between the lines, using clues from text and pictures, to discuss thoughts, feelings and actions?
> (ORCS Standard 3, 23)

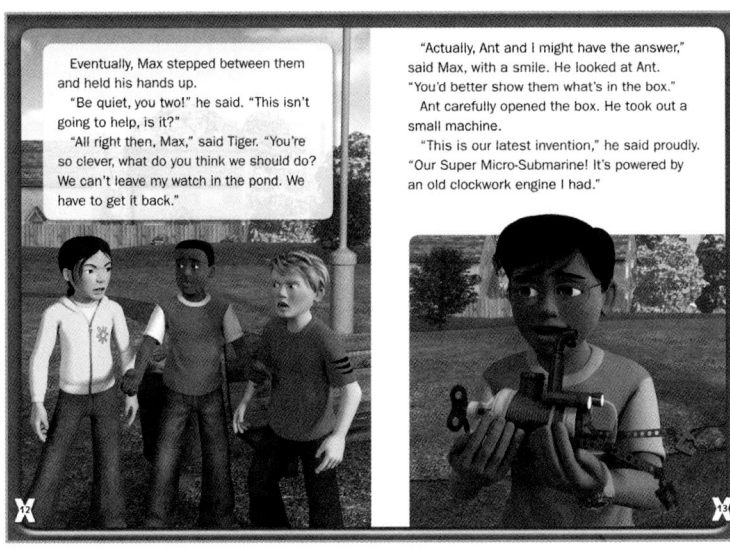

Developing grammar, punctuation and spelling

- Ask the children to carry out a detective hunt to collect words that show which person (first and third) the story is written in.
- Give the children the *First and third person words* Photocopy Master to help them sort first and third person words.
- Ask the children to use a computer to write a scene from *Underwater Adventure* in the third person in their own words. Then ask them to highlight all the third person words in green on the screen.
- Read the second paragraph on page 13 again. Ask the children what tense this is written in. How do they know? (The verbs are in the past tense, e.g. *opened*.) Now look at the dialogue on the page. What tense is this written in (present)?
- Ask the children to flick through the book again and identify where past tense and present tense are used in the story. Explain that stories are usually written in the past tense but speech will often be written in the present tense.
- Write the words *metal* and *special* on the board and ask the children for the sound that they can hear in each. Discuss how the /l/ sound is sometimes spelt 'al' at the end of words. Can they think of any other examples? How else might this sound be spelt?

Assessment point
Can the children talk about how different words and phrases affect meaning?
(ORCS Standard 3, 21)

Follow-up

Writing activities

- Ask the children to choose a page of text in the story and help them to turn it into the first person. Which kinds of words did they have to change? **(short writing task)**
- Using their ideas from their earlier role play, ask the children to write a story showing how Tiger might save Max and Ant. Remind the children to write the story in the third person. **(longer writing task)**
- Ask the children to use the *My invention* Photocopy Master to draw and describe an invention of their own that they could use to help someone. **(short writing task)**

Other literacy activities

- Ask the children, in small groups, to retell consecutive chapters to each other in their own words. **(spoken language)**

Cross-curricular activities

- Design an underwater vehicle. **(DT)**
- Explore pond habitats to see what other pond life the children in the story might have seen. **(Science)**
- Explore how people's comments make others feel and link this to how Tiger feels when everyone keeps saying he breaks things. **(PSHE)**

Cuckoo Trouble
BY TONY BRADMAN

Curricular correlation
English National Curriculum

Spoken language	Use relevant strategies to build their vocabulary
Word reading	Read accurately by blending the sounds in words that contain the graphemes taught so far, especially recognising alternative sounds for graphemes
Comprehension	Discussing and clarifying the meanings of words, linking new meanings to known vocabulary
	Discuss their favourite words and phrases
	Predict what might happen on the basis of what has been read so far

Phonics and vocabulary

GPCs	/ai/ amazing, explain, playing, escape, break, straight, weight /ee/ he, weeds, reveal, grease, piece /or/ for, claw, launched, thought
Decodable 2 and 3 syllable words	ticking, darkness, window
Common exception words	friends, can't, inside, food, through, thought, going, know, pulled, find, climb, door, hour
Challenge and context words	cuckoo, invention, says, idea, busy, whirring, once, wrong, answer, thought, weights, sign

Grammar, punctuation and spelling

Grammar and Punctuation	How the grammatical patterns in a sentence indicate its function as a statement, question, exclamation or command	"The clock is on the wall behind them." (statement) "Why didn't you say that in the first place?" (question) "Oh, no!" (exclamation) "Wait, Tiger!" (command)
Spelling	Adding the endings -ing, -ed and -er to a root word ending in -y with a consonant before it	trying, tied, cried easier, earlier

Reading assessment points (Oxford Reading Criterion Scale: Assessment Standard 3)

3. Can the children apply phonic skills and knowledge to recognize an increasing number of complex words? (READ)
7. Can the children make predictions about a text using a range of clues? (D)
9. Can the children provide simple explanations about events or information? (D)
15. Can the children read aloud with intonation, taking into account a wider range of punctuation (. ? ! ,)? (READ)
17. Can the children explain the meaning of 'WOW' words in context? (D)
21. Can the children talk about how different words and phrases affect meaning? (E)

Scottish Curriculum for Excellence

Listening and talking	I am explaining how pace, gesture, expression, emphasis and choice of words are used to engage others, and I can use what I learn ENG 1-03a
Reading	I can use my knowledge of sight vocabulary, phonics, context clues, punctuation and grammar to read with understanding and expression ENG 1-12a
	I can share my thoughts about structure, characters and/or setting, recognise the writer's message and relate it to my own experiences, and comment on the effective choice of words and other features ENG 1-19a
	To show my understanding across different areas of learning, I can identify and consider the purpose and main ideas of a text LIT 1-16a

Foundation Phase Framework in Wales

Oracy	Express opinions, giving reasons, and provide appropriate answers to questions (Speaking)
	Speak clearly to a range of audiences (Speaking)
Reading	Apply the following reading strategies with increasing frequency to a range of familiar and unfamiliar texts: phonic strategies; recognition of HFW; context clues, e.g. prior knowledge; graphic and syntactic clues; self-correction, including re-reading and reading ahead (Reading strategies)
	Read aloud with attention to punctuation, including full stops, question, exclamation and speech marks, varying intonation, voice and pace (Reading strategies)
	Show understanding and express opinions about language, information and events in texts (Response and analysis)
	Express views about information and details in a text (Response and analysis)

Northern Ireland Curriculum

Talking and Listening	Think about what they say and how they say it
Reading	Use a range of strategies to identify unfamiliar words
	Use a range of comprehension skills, both oral and written, to interpret and discuss texts

About this book

This story follows on from *Underwater Adventure* and shows Tiger using his ingenuity to help rescue Max and Ant from the bottom of the pond.

You will need

- *Long vowel hunt* Photocopy Master, *Teaching Handbook* for Year 2/P3
- *What can you see, hear, smell?* Photocopy Master, *Teaching Handbook* for Year 2/P3
- *Story board* Photocopy Master, *Teaching Handbook* for Year 2/P3

> Before reading

- Ask the children to recap what happened in the previous story *Underwater Adventure*. **(recall, summarizing)**
- Compare the children's versions of the previous story with the summary on pages 2 and 3. Are there any main points they have missed? **(recall)**
- How do they think Tiger is going to save the boys? **(predicting)**
- Ask the children what to do if they encounter a difficult word, modelling with an example from the book.
- Discuss with the children what to do if they struggle to understand the meaning of a word or a sentence, e.g. rereading the word or sentence again.

Assessment point

Can the children make predictions about a text using a range of clues? (ORCS Standard 3, 7)

Phonic opportunity

- Draw attention to words with the /**ai**/, /**ee**/ and /**or**/ phonemes. Ask the children to identify these GPCs in the words. Support children to say each phoneme and then blend the phonemes to read the word. Give out the *Long vowel hunt* Photocopy Master and ask the children to be word detectives and hunt through the book to find words with these long vowels.
- You may also wish to point out some of the common exception words or practise decoding some of the challenge and context words in this book.

Assessment point
Can the children apply phonic skills and knowledge to recognize an increasing number of complex words? (ORCS Standard 3, 3)

During reading

- Ask the children to read from page 4 to the end of the book.
- As they read, ask them to notice how the author uses language and descriptive phases to interest the reader, e.g. *"We can climb up the bookcase and then swing across to the clock using the wool like a rope!"* (p.12).
- Also ask the children to look out for words with the *-ing*, *-ed* and *-er* suffixes.

After reading

Returning to the text

- Why were Cat and Tiger relieved that Moggy was not in the room? **(deducing, inferring, drawing conclusions)**
- Ask the children how Cat and Tiger managed to get up the bookcase. **(recall)**
- Look at the phrase *"It's as high as a mountain!"* on page 11. Why do they think the author used this phrase? How does it help the reader to imagine the setting? **(determining importance)**
- Are there any other descriptive words and phrases that they particularly like?

Assessment point
Can the children provide simple explanations about events or information? (ORCS Standard 3, 9)

Developing comprehension

- The author has decided to help the reader to imagine what it is like by describing what the children could see, hear and smell inside the cuckoo clock. How does this help the reader to imagine a scene? **(synthesizing)**
- Talk about the descriptive words and phrases the children discovered in their reading. Which ones did they like? How did the vocabulary help them to picture the story in their mind? Did any words and phrases evoke particular feelings such as fear or excitement?
- Did the children notice any devices the author used, such as the use of onomatopoeic words (*tick-tick-ticking*, p.16) and placing words in capitals and italics (*BOINNNNNGGGG!*, p.19)?
- Ask the children to complete the *What can you see, hear, smell?* Photocopy Master to describe what it might be like if you could shrink and find yourself inside another everyday household object, e.g. a vacuum cleaner, refrigerator, food cupboard, etc. Challenge the children to use descriptive words and phrases. **(visualizing and other sensory responses)**

Assessment point
Can the children explain the meaning of 'WOW' words in context (appropriate level of book), e.g. despair, marvel (including words with common prefixes and suffixes e.g. undecided, forgetful)? (ORCS Standard 3, 17)

Assessment point
Can the children talk about how different words and phrases affect meaning? (ORCS Standard 3, 21)

Developing grammar, punctuation and spelling

- Turn to pages 6–8 and ask the children to identify a statement, exclamation, question and command on these pages. Discuss the punctuation that is used for each and the words that help indicate the sentence type. Give each child a double-page spread of their own to look at and identify the types of sentence on each. Give time for each child to explain their conclusions to the rest of the group.

- Look at the words the children have collected with the *-ing*, *-ed* or *-er* suffix. Look at the examples they've found where there is an 'i' before these suffixes. Discuss the spelling rule: if a word ends in consonant-y you need to change the 'y' to an 'i' before adding *-ed* or *-er*. Explain that this rule does not apply to adding *-ing* to words that end in this way. Instead *-ing* is simply added to the end of the word (e.g. *trying*)

Developing fluency

- Ask the children, in turn, to read aloud a page each of Chapters 4 and 5, reminding them to build up the tension in the story through the use of their voice.

Assessment point

Can the children read aloud with intonation, taking into account a wider range of punctuation (. ? ! ,)? (ORCS Standard 3, 15)

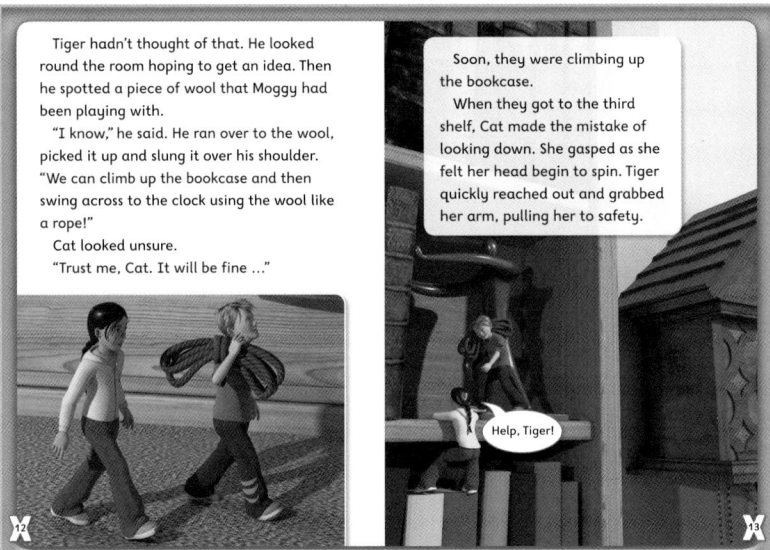

Follow-up

Writing activities

- Ask the children to write speech bubbles for the characters in some of the pictures, then compare them with a partner's. **(short writing task)**
- Ask the children to use their description of a setting to begin a longer imaginative story about a person who shrinks in order to rescue someone. They could use the *Story board* Photocopy Master to help them plan the story. **(longer writing task)**
- Look at how the author has used the word *Meanwhile* (p.20) to allow the reader to find out what is happening to the other characters in the story. Read short sections of the story to the children again, then end the section with the word *Meanwhile* ... . Ask the children to write what might be going on at this point with the other characters in the story. **(short writing task)**

Other literacy activities

- Ask the children to invent another plan to rescue Max and Ant. Invite them to describe their plan to a partner, who will then explain to someone else how the plan works. Encourage the children to focus on giving precise and clear instructions. **(spoken language)**

Cross-curricular activities

- Explore pattern and design using cogs and wheels. **(Art and Design)**
- Explore ways of making the sounds of a cuckoo clock. Encourage the children to make both loud and soft sounds. **(Science)**
- Investigate the mechanisms used in clocks. **(DT)**

Ant and the Break-bot

BY CHRIS POWLING

Curricular correlation

English National Curriculum

Spoken language	Give well-structured descriptions and explanations
Word reading	Read further common exception words, noting unusual correspondence between spelling and sound
Comprehension	Discuss the sequence of events in books and how items of information are related
	Make inferences on the basis of what is being said and done
	Draw on what they already know or on background information provided by the teacher

Phonics and vocabulary

GPCs	/s/ special, pressed, cinema, dance /ee/ free, maybe, reading, completely, Katie, curtsey, Lucy, Beauty-bot
Decodable 2 and 3 syllable words	competition, tickets, robot, Spangler, plastic, finished
Common exception words	never, first, couldn't, garden, everyone, around
Challenge and context words	break-dance, movie, build, awesome, whispered, guys, laughter, busy, judges, cinema, wrong

Grammar, punctuation and spelling

Grammar and Punctuation	Expanded noun phrases for description and specification	latest Robo-Rex movie; opening night; big stars; best robot; sleek, shiny, pink robot
Spelling	The /ur/ sound spelt 'or' after 'w'	worked, worry, word

Reading assessment points (Oxford Reading Criterion Scale: Assessment Standard 3)

1. Can the children identify when reading does not make sense and self-correct in order for the text to make sense? (READ)
6. Can the children locate some specific information e.g. key events, characters' names etc. or key information on a non-fiction page? (R)
18. Can the children summarise a story, giving the main points clearly in sequence? (R)
21. Can the children talk about how different words and phrases affect meaning? (E)
23. Are the children beginning to read between the lines, using clues from text and pictures, to discuss thoughts, feelings and actions? (D)
24. Can the children confidently relate texts to their own experiences? (D)

Scottish Curriculum for Excellence

Listening and talking	When I engage with others, I know when and how to listen, when to talk, how much to say, when to ask questions and how to respond with respect LIT 1-02a
Reading	I can use my knowledge of sight vocabulary, phonics, context clues, punctuation and grammar to read with understanding and expression ENG 1-12a
	I can share my thoughts about structure, characters and/or setting, recognise the writer's message and relate it to my own experiences, and comment on the effective choice of words and other features ENG 1-19a
	To show my understanding across different areas of learning, I can identify and consider the purpose and main ideas of a text LIT 1-16a

Foundation Phase Framework in Wales

Oracy	Express opinions, giving reasons, and provide appropriate answers to questions (Speaking)
	Share activities and information to complete a task (Collaboration)
Reading	Apply the following reading strategies with increasing frequency to a range of familiar and unfamiliar texts: phonic strategies; recognition of HFW; context clues, e.g. prior knowledge; graphic and syntactic clues; self-correction, including re-reading and reading ahead (Reading strategies)
	Show understanding and express opinions about language, information and events in texts (Reading strategies)
	Explain relevant details from texts (Comprehension)

Northern Ireland Curriculum

Talking and Listening	Take turns at talking and listening in group and paired activities
Reading	Use a range of strategies to identify unfamiliar words
	Begin to use evidence from text to support their views
	Express opinions and give reasons based on what they have read

Ant and the Break-bot

About this book

The children have the chance to win free tickets to see the new Robo-Rex film, if they can build an amazing robot. Ant has an idea to build a robot that can break-dance, like himself. Max, Cat and Tiger shrink to help him operate the robot, but disaster strikes on the day of the competition.

You will need
- *Ant's email* Photocopy Master, *Teaching Handbook* for Year 2/P3

❯ Before reading

- Talk to the children about entering competitions. Have they ever entered a competition? How did it feel being a competitor? **(activating prior knowledge)**
- Take a picture walk through the story. What challenges do the characters meet? Do they think, based on the pictures, that the story will have a happy ending? **(previewing the text, predicting)**
- Look at page 2 and then read the first chapter to the children. Use intonation to build excitement and tension and ask the children to imitate your style of reading by rereading the same section aloud. **(engaging readers, developing fluency)**
- Ask the children what to do if they encounter a difficult word, modelling with an example from the book.
- Discuss with the children what to do if they struggle to understand the meaning of a word or a sentence, e.g. rereading the word or sentence again.

Assessment point
Can the children confidently relate texts to their own experiences? (ORCS Standard 3, 24)

Assessment point
Can the children identify when reading does not make sense and self-correct in order for the text to make sense? (ORCS Standard 3, 1)

> *Phonic opportunity*

- Draw attention to words with the **/s/** phoneme: *special, pressed, cinema, dance*. Ask children to identify the GPC /s/ in the words. Support children to say each phoneme and then blend the phonemes to read the word.
- Now look at words with the **/ee/** phoneme: *free, maybe, reading, completely, Katie, curtsey, Lucy, Beauty-bot*.
- Alternatively, depending on the phonic work you have been undertaking, select one or two of the words from the book and remind the children how to say and blend phonemes.
- You may wish to point out some of the common exception words or practise decoding some of the challenge and context words in this book.

During reading

- Ask the children to read from Chapter 2 to the end of the book.
- As they read, ask them to note what was special about Lucy's robot.

Assessment point
Can the children locate some specific information e.g. key events, characters' names etc. or key information on a non-fiction page?
(ORCS Standard 3, 6)

After reading

Returning to the text

- What robot had Lucy designed and what special attributes did it have? **(recall)**
- How was Ant's Break-bot powered? **(recall)**
- Referring to the text, why didn't Ant's Break-bot win? **(recall, deducing, inferring, drawing conclusions)**
- Why do they think the competition organizers decided to award Ant a prize after all? **(synthesizing)**

Assessment point
Are the children beginning to read between the lines, using clues from text and pictures, to discuss thoughts, feelings and actions?
(ORCS Standard 3, 23)

Developing comprehension

- Ask the children to draw a large circle, divide it into six sections – the number of chapters in the book – then write each chapter heading above one of the sections. The children then complete the summary wheel for the story by noting down the key events in the sections under the chapter headings. **(summarizing)**

- Using their notes, ask the children, in pairs, to take a chapter in turn and retell the story to each other. Encourage them to use story language as much as possible. **(recall, summarizing, determining importance, visualizing)**

- Look at the email on page 31. Using *Ant's email* Photocopy Master, ask the children to write an email to the judges. Discuss some possible responses Ant might give. Remind them why it is important to fill in the 'To' and 'Subject' fields.

Assessment point
Can the children summarise a story, giving the main points clearly in sequence?
(ORCS Standard 3, 18)

Chapter 4 – Strictly come robot-ing

The cinema was packed with children and robots. At the front, there was a model of Robo-Rex. Three judges were also on the stage, sitting behind a big desk. They were looking down at everyone.

"They make me nervous," said micro-size Tiger. Tiger was hidden in the leg of the robot. Cat was working the arms. Max was in the head.

"Don't worry," whispered Ant. "When we're dancing, just do what I do."

Ant looked around the room. He spotted Lucy, a girl from school. She was a show-off. A crowd of people were standing around her. She was holding a sleek, shiny, pink robot.

"What's so special about her robot?" Cat wondered.

"Nothing to worry about," Ant whispered to his friends inside Break-bot.

"Are you sure?" Max said, peering through Break-bot's eyes.

Developing grammar, punctuation and spelling

- Write the word *robot* on the board and ask children to explain what picture they have in their heads. Now write *sleek, shiny, pink robot* on the board and ask them how their image has changed. Discuss how the expanded noun phrase adds detail and makes the information more specific for the reader. Discuss how this helps the reader to visualize the noun more precisely. Challenge children to look through the book and identify other examples of expanded noun phrases that add specific details.

- Write the words *worked* and *worry* on the board and ask the children for the sound that they can hear in each. Discuss how the /ur/ sound is sometimes spelt with an 'or' after a 'w'. Can they think of any other examples?

Assessment point
Can the children talk about how different words and phrases affect meaning?
(ORCS Standard 3, 21)

Developing fluency

- Ask the children to take on the role of one of the main characters. Go through the story together and ask them to rehearse the dialogue for their character, trying to ensure they use appropriate expression and intonation to bring out the meaning of the words.

▶ Follow-up

Writing activities

- Ask the children to look at their favourite section in the story and change some of the dialogue of the characters to thought bubbles. How does the text and punctuation need to change? **(short writing task)**
- Write an email inviting people to enter a competition to design a robot. The children will need to explain what sort of robots they are looking for, what the prize will be, and so on. **(longer writing task)**
- Ask the children to design and draw a robot. Ask them to label its features and write a short description about what makes their robot special. **(short writing task)**

Other literacy activities

- Create your own class competition for designing a robot. Give each member of the group or class roles to carry out. Promote the competition with posters and adverts, appoint judges, give feedback to entrants and work as a team.

Cross-curricular activities

- Work as a group to plan, design and build a giant robot. **(DT)**
- In small groups, the children could research one break-dancing move on the Internet and attempt to practise and perform it to the class. **(PE)**

Flying Machines
BY JOHN MALAM

Curricular correlation
English National Curriculum

Spoken language	Use spoken language to develop understanding through speculating, hypothesising, imagining and exploring ideas
Word reading	Read aloud books closely matched to their improving phonic knowledge, sounding out unfamiliar words accurately, automatically and without undue hesitation
Comprehension	Check that the text makes sense to them as they read and correcting inaccurate reading
	Read non-fiction books that are structured in different ways
	Ask and answer questions

Phonics and vocabulary

GPCs	/igh/ idea, flight, fly, died, spitfire, height /or/ story, before, four
Decodable 2 and 3 syllable words	inventor, helicopter, hundred, propeller, enemy, factory, notebooks, airstrip, airshows
Common exception words	why, when, would, after, before, began, birds, fly
Challenge and context words	ancient, ideas, machines, built, fuselage, bicycles, soldier, ammunition, fuel, floods, weird, stealth, aerial, journey, designed

Grammar, punctuation and spelling

Grammar and Punctuation	Commas to separate items in a list	soldiers, weapons, ammunition and fuel are moved by Chinooks.
Spelling	Adding -es to nouns and verbs ending in -y	flies, carries, countries

Reading assessment points (Oxford Reading Criterion Scale: Assessment Standard 3)

3.	Can the children apply phonic skills and knowledge to recognize an increasing number of complex words? (READ)
5.	Can the children confidently recognize a range of patterns in texts, including stories, poems and non-fiction, e.g. use of simple common features of non-fiction texts? (A)
15.	Can the children read aloud with intonation, taking into account a wider range of punctuation (. ? ! ,)? (READ)
19.	Can the children distinguish between fiction and non-fiction? (A)
20.	Having read a text, can the children find the answers to questions, both written and oral? (R)
25.	Can the children talk about the features of certain non-fiction texts (non-chronological report, recount, letter)? (A)
26.	Can the children demonstrate how to use information books? (R/A)

Scottish Curriculum for Excellence

Listening and talking	I can show my understanding of what I listen to or watch by responding to and asking different kinds of questions LIT 1-07a
Reading	I can use my knowledge of sight vocabulary, phonics, context clues, punctuation and grammar to read with understanding and expression ENG 1-12a
	I am learning to select and use strategies and resources before I read, and as I read, to help make the meaning of texts clear LIT 1-13a
	Using what I know about the features of different types of texts, I can find, select, sort and use information for a specific purpose LIT 1-14a
	I can share my thoughts about structure, characters and/or setting, recognise the writer's message and relate it to my own experiences, and comment on the effective choice of words and other features ENG 1-19a

Foundation Phase Framework in Wales

Oracy	Express opinions, giving reasons, and provide appropriate answers to questions (Speaking)
	Show understanding of what they have heard by asking relevant questions to find out specific information (Listening)
Reading	Apply the following reading strategies with increasing frequency to a range of familiar and unfamiliar texts: phonic strategies; recognition of HFW; context clues, e.g. prior knowledge; graphic and syntactic clues; self-correction, including re-reading and reading ahead (Reading strategies)
	Use the different features of texts to make meaning, e.g. pictures, charts, and layout (Reading strategies)
	Show understanding and express opinions about language, information and events in texts (Response and analysis)

Northern Ireland Curriculum

Talking and Listening	Devise and ask questions to find information in social situations and across the curriculum
Reading	Use a range of strategies to identify unfamiliar words
	Begin to locate, select and use texts for specific purposes
	Use a range of comprehension skills, both oral and written, to interpret and discuss texts

About this book
This non-fiction book looks at the history of flight from Leonardo da Vinci's ideas of flying machines to modern planes that fly into space.

You will need
- *Flying phonemes* Photocopy Master, *Teaching Handbook* for Year 2/P3
- *Help wanted!* Photocopy Master, *Teaching Handbook* for Year 2/P3

▶ Before reading

- What different flying machines do the children know about? Give them a large piece of paper to share and ask them to begin a concept map that shows what they already know about flying machines. **(activating prior knowledge)**

  Assessment point
  Can the children distinguish between fiction and non-fiction? (ORCS Standard 3, 19)

- What type of book is *Flying Machines*? **(activating prior knowledge)**
- Look at the section headings on the contents page. Can the children use the headings to discuss what information about flying machines they might find in the book? **(previewing the text, predicting)**
- Ask the children what to do if they encounter a difficult word, modelling with an example from the book.
- Discuss with the children what to do if they struggle to understand the meaning of a word or a sentence, e.g. rereading the word or sentence again.

Phonic opportunity

- Draw attention to words with the /**igh**/ phoneme: *idea, flight, fly, died, spitfire, height*. Ask children to identify the GPC /igh/ in the words. Support children to say each phoneme and then blend the phonemes to read the word.
- Now look at words with the /or/ phoneme: *story, before, four*.
- Give the children the *Flying phonemes* Photocopy Master. Ask them to cut out the cards with the unusual names on them and use their phoneme knowledge to try to read them. The children can then check the pronunciation of the names in the book.
- You may also wish to point out some of the common exception words or practise decoding some of the challenge and context words in this book.

Assessment point
Can the children apply phonic skills and knowledge to recognize an increasing number of complex words?
(ORCS Standard 3, 3)

During reading

- Ask the children to choose two sections from the contents page that most interest them to read.
- When they have finished reading these sections, ask them to use the index to find information about different subjects quickly. For example, can they find information about Charles Kettering or the Stealth Bomber?
- Ask the children to look out for words with the *-es* suffix as they read.

Assessment point
Can the children demonstrate how to use information books?
(ORCS Standard 3, 26)

After reading

Returning to the text

- Ask the children why they chose the particular sections they did. **(personal response)**
- Did they enjoy the sections? Why or why not? **(personal response, adopting a critical stance)**
- What do they notice about the index? Is it in a particular order? **(recall)**
- What different information features did they find on their pages? How useful were they? **(synthesizing)**
- What new information have they found out about flying? **(summarizing)**

Assessment point
Can the children talk about the features of certain non-fiction texts (non-chronological report, recount, letter)?
(ORCS Standard 3, 25)

Developing comprehension

- Ask the children to revisit the concept maps they began at the beginning of the book. What new information can they add to the map? **(synthesizing)**
- Ask the children to work together to develop other questions that they would like to find out about flying machines. Encourage them to listen to each other's questions and then make a final list of questions that would be the most useful to research. **(questioning)**
- Ask the children to use their knowledge gained from reading this book to create a section about flying machines. The section should include a range of non-fiction features such as charts, captions and bullet points.

Assessment point
Having read a text, can the children find the answers to questions, both written and oral?
(ORCS Standard 3, 20)

Assessment point
Can the children confidently recognize a range of patterns in texts, including stories, poems and non-fiction, e.g. use of simple common features of non-fiction texts?
(ORCS Standard 3, 5)

Developing vocabulary

- Ask the children to look up some of the emboldened words in the glossary. Can they find any other words in the text they think could go in the glossary, e.g. *glider, mission, unmanned*? Together, you could create glossary definitions for these words.

Developing grammar, punctuation and spelling

- Write the following sentence on the board: *soldiers, weapons, ammunition and fuel are moved by Chinooks*. Can they identify the punctuation mark that appears twice here? Discuss that it is a comma and it can be used to separate things in a list.
- Look at the words the children have collected with the *-es* suffix. Look at the examples they've found where there is an 'i' before the *-es*. Discuss the spelling rule: if a noun or a verb ends in consonant-y you need to change the 'y' to an 'i' before adding *-es*. Can they think of other words that would follow this rule?

Developing fluency

- Invite the children to reread one of their chosen sections aloud to help the rest of the group understand the information.

Assessment point

Can the children read aloud with intonation, taking into account a wider range of punctuation (. ? ! ,)? (ORCS Standard 3, 15)

Follow-up

Writing activities

- Ask the children to complete the concept map about flying machines. **(short writing task)**
- Give out the *Help wanted* Photocopy Master to the children and ask them to list other words/information from the book that could be added to the index. They then need to write the page number where the information can be found. The children could swap their indexes with a partner to see if they were correct. **(short writing task)**
- Encourage the children to research the list of questions they created using books and the Internet. They could then each write a section, adding the information they have discovered. Later on, the group could compile an index for their completed sections. **(longer writing task)**

Other literacy activities

- Delegate sections of the book to different pairs of children. Ask them to read the information in their section quietly together, then bring the group together and invite members to ask each other questions about the sections. **(spoken language)**

Cross-curricular activities

- Design a flying machine, ensuring that it has some features to enable it to fly, such as propellers. The children could invent an appropriate name for it. **(DT)**
- Design an image for a kite. **(Art and Design)**
- Use a globe to identify the countries that are mentioned in the book. **(Geography)**
- Investigate the birds that live in the local environment. Ask children to identify and name them. **(Science)**

Extreme Exploring Machines
BY ALISON BLANK

Curricular correlation

English National Curriculum

Spoken language	Ask relevant questions to extend their understanding and build vocabulary and knowledge
Word reading	Read aloud books closely matched to their improving phonic knowledge, sounding out unfamiliar words accurately, automatically and without undue hesitation
Comprehension	Answer and ask questions
	Read non-fiction books that are structured in different ways
	Explain and discuss their understanding of books

Phonics and vocabulary

GPCs	/**ai**/ volcano, contain, layers, x-ray, days, earthquake, safely, lake /**dj**/ engineer, geothermal, wreckage, July, journey
Decodable 2 and 3 syllable words	robot, toxic, explorer, volcanic, amazing, equipment, Titanic, underwater, onboard
Common exception words	many, water, inside, find, which, once, where
Challenge and context words	tsunamis, ocean, floor, machines, scientists, build, learn, signs, wheels, ice, tough, dangerous, engineer

Grammar, punctuation and spelling

Grammar and Punctuation	Use of capital letters, full stops, question marks and exclamation marks to demarcate sentences	How can humans explore below the ice in Antarctica? There are some places that are too difficult and dangerous for humans to visit. Over five years later, it is still working there!
Spelling	The /r/ sound spelt 'wr' at the beginning of words	wreckage, wrapped

Reading assessment points (Oxford Reading Criterion Scale: Assessment Standard 3)

1.	Can the children identify when reading does not make sense and self-correct in order for the text to make sense? (READ)
6.	Can the children locate some specific information, e.g. key information in a non-fiction text? (R)
7.	Can the children make predictions about a text using a range of clues? (D)
15.	Can the children read aloud with intonation, taking into account a wider range of punctuation (. ? ! ,)? (READ)
23.	Are the children beginning to read between the lines, using clues from text and pictures, to discuss thoughts, feelings and actions? (D)
26.	Can the children demonstrate how to use information books? (R/A)

Scottish Curriculum for Excellence

Listening and talking	I can show my understanding of what I listen to or watch by responding to and asking different kinds of questions LIT 1-07a
Reading	I can use my knowledge of sight vocabulary, phonics, context clues, punctuation and grammar to read with understanding and expression ENG 1-12a
	To show my understanding, I can respond to different kinds of questions and other close reading tasks and I am learning to create some questions of my own ENG 1-17a
	I am learning to select and use strategies and resources before I read, and as I read, to help make the meaning of texts clear LIT 1-13a
	To show my understanding across different areas of learning, I can identify and consider the purpose and main ideas of a text LIT 1-16a

Foundation Phase Framework in Wales

Oracy	Express opinions, giving reasons, and provide appropriate answers to questions (Speaking)
	Show understanding of what they have heard by asking relevant questions to find out specific information (Listening)
Reading	Apply the following reading strategies with increasing frequency to a range of familiar and unfamiliar texts: phonic strategies; recognition of HFW; context clues, e.g. prior knowledge; graphic and syntactic clues; self-correction, including re-reading and reading ahead (Reading strategies)
	Make links between texts read and new information about the topic (Comprehension)
	Express views about information and details in a text (Response and analysis)

Northern Ireland Curriculum

Talking and Listening	Listen to, interpret and retell, with some supporting detail, a range of oral and written texts
Reading	Use a range of strategies to identify unfamiliar words
	Use a range of comprehension skills, both oral and written, to interpret and discuss texts

Extreme Exploring Machines

About this book
This book describes how new inventions have been developed to explore extreme environments.

You will need
- *Explore or not to explore?* Photocopy Master, *Teaching Handbook* for Year 2/P3 (enlarged)
- *Compare and contrast information* Photocopy Master, *Teaching Handbook* for Year 2/P3 *(Year 2/P3)*
- Books/films/magazines/web links on environments mentioned in the book, e.g. volcanoes, planets (Mars), ocean floor, Antarctica (optional)

▶ Before reading

- Look at the front cover. What do the children think the image might be of? **(predicting)**
- Look at the section headings on the contents page. Which extreme place would they most like to explore? Why? **(activating prior knowledge, personal response)**
- If possible, give the children the opportunity to look at books, films, pictures and websites to help them to get to know some of the places that are explored in the book. Provide small world materials to allow them to explore their own worlds. **(building prior knowledge)**
- Read pages 2 and 3 to the children. Demonstrate leaving pauses after reading a question to allow the listener to think about the questions being posed. What other questions would the children like to ask? **(developing fluency, engaging readers)**
- Ask the children what to do if they encounter a difficult word, modelling with an example from the book.
- Discuss with the children what to do if they struggle to understand the meaning of a word or a sentence, e.g. rereading the word or sentence again.

Assessment point
Can the children make predictions about a text using a range of clues? (ORCS Standard 3, 7)

Assessment point
Can the children identify when reading does not make sense and self-correct in order for the text to make sense? (ORCS Standard 3, 1)

> *Phonic opportunity*

- Draw attention to words with the /**ai**/ phoneme: *volcano, contain, layers, x-ray, days, earthquake, safely, lake*. Ask children to identify the GPC /ai/ in the words. Support children to say each phoneme and then blend the phonemes to read the word.
- Now look at words with the /**dj**/ phoneme: *engineer, geothermal, wreckage, July, journey*.
- Alternatively, depending on the phonic work you have been undertaking, select one or two of the words from the book and remind the children how to say and blend phonemes.
- You may wish to point out some of the common exceptional words or practise decoding some of the challenge and context words in this book.

During reading

- Ask the children to choose three sections from the contents page that they would like to read. Explain that they will also need to read the final section on page 22.
- As they read, ask them to think of any questions they would like to ask an expert. Remind them to look carefully at the labelled diagrams as a source of information.
- As they read, ask the children to look out for how sentences begin and end, e.g. capital letters, full stops and question marks.

Assessment point
Can the children demonstrate how to use information books?
(ORCS Standard 3, 26)

After reading

Returning to the text

- Ask the children what made them choose the sections they did. **(personal response, adopting a critical stance)**
- Can the children remember what each extreme exploring machine was used for? **(recall, summarizing)**
- Where is Lake Vostok? Why do the children think the author has raised the issue of whether these types of lakes should be explored? **(deducing, inferring, drawing conclusions, personal response, adopting a critical stance)**
- Using an enlarged copy of the *Explore or not to explore?* Photocopy Master ask the children to contribute arguments towards whether or not scientists should explore extreme environments. Write the arguments under the headings and ask the children, as a group, to decide on the best wording to use. **(synthesizing, personal response, adopting a critical stance)**
- Depending on each child's viewpoint, ask them to write a short letter to NASA to persuade them to design a new machine to explore a different planet, or stop exploring new places to avoid damaging the Earth. Remind them to use or adapt the arguments that you listed as a group.

> **Assessment point**
> Are the children beginning to read between the lines, using clues from text and pictures, to discuss thoughts, feelings and actions?
> (ORCS Standard 3, 23)

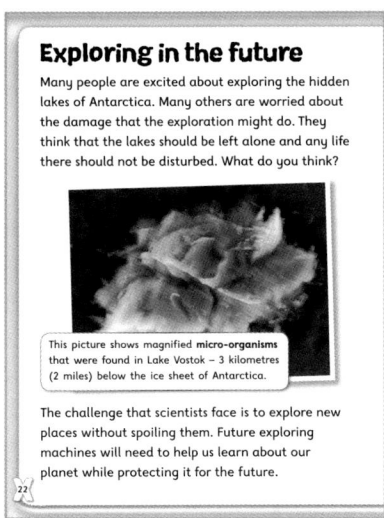

Exploring in the future

Many people are excited about exploring the hidden lakes of Antarctica. Many others are worried about the damage that the exploration might do. They think that the lakes should be left alone and any life there should not be disturbed. What do you think?

This picture shows magnified **micro-organisms** that were found in Lake Vostok – 3 kilometres (2 miles) below the ice sheet of Antarctica.

The challenge that scientists face is to explore new places without spoiling them. Future exploring machines will need to help us learn about our planet while protecting it for the future.

Developing comprehension

- Ask the children to think of questions they would like to ask an expert to find out more about the unusual environments they have explored. **(questioning)**
- Allow them to choose the environment they are most interested in and provide them with books, magazines and web links to explore the environment in greater depth. Ask the children to complete a *Compare and contrast information* Photocopy Master, listing the different sources they have used. **(synthesizing)**
- What new environments do the children think might be left to discover? **(predicting)**

Assessment point
Can the children locate some specific information, e.g. key information in a non-fiction text?
(ORCS Standard 3, 6)

Developing grammar, punctuation and spelling

- Write some of the sentences from the book on the board and remind the children of the importance of using capital letters and full stops in sentences. When might they replace a full stop with a question mark or an exclamation mark?
- Look specifically at the labelled diagrams. Why do some end with a full stop and others don't?
- Write the words *wreckage* and *wrapped* on the board and ask children for the sound that they can hear in each. Discuss how the /r/ sound is sometimes spelt 'wr' at the start of words. Can they think of any other examples?

Assessment point
Can the children read aloud with intonation, taking into account a wider range of punctuation (. ? ! ,)?
(ORCS Standard 3, 15)

> Follow-up

Writing activities

- Write a short description of an imaginary super machine that has been designed to explore a new extreme environment. Give the machine an appropriate name. **(short writing task)**
- Create a labelled diagram of the super machine, giving technical information about it. They could use the captions for the diagram on pages 6 and 7 as a model for the style of writing. **(short writing task)**
- Ask the children to use their notes on the *Compare and contrast information* Photocopy Master to compile an information text about their chosen extreme environment. These could be displayed in the classroom for other children to read. **(longer writing task)**

Other literacy activities

- Work as a group to create a TV broadcast describing the day your new super machine is used to explore an extreme environment. Ensure each member of the group has a role and works as part of a team. **(spoken language)**

Cross-curricular activities

- Design a machine to explore a different environment, e.g. a mountain terrain, underground cave, or a planet other than Mars. **(DT)**
- Find out about famous explorers such as Christopher Columbus or Neil Armstrong **(History)**